YOUR KNOWLEDGE HAS VALUE

AF135858

- We will publish your bachelor's and master's thesis, essays and papers

- Your own eBook and book - sold worldwide in all relevant shops

- Earn money with each sale

Upload your text at www.GRIN.com and publish for free

Bibliographic information published by the German National Library:

The German National Library lists this publication in the National Bibliography; detailed bibliographic data are available on the Internet at http://dnb.dnb.de .

Imprint:

Copyright © 2019 GRIN Verlag
Print and binding: Books on Demand GmbH, Norderstedt Germany
ISBN: 9783346095435

This book at GRIN:

https://www.grin.com/document/512216

Natasha Shroff

Aus der Reihe: e-fellows.net stipendiaten-wissen

e-fellows.net (Hrsg.)

Band 3317

Detecting and reducing loneliness. Introducing quality communication into lives of elderly

GRIN Verlag

GRIN - Your knowledge has value

Since its foundation in 1998, GRIN has specialized in publishing academic texts by students, college teachers and other academics as e-book and printed book. The website www.grin.com is an ideal platform for presenting term papers, final papers, scientific essays, dissertations and specialist books.

Visit us on the internet:

http://www.grin.com/

http://www.facebook.com/grincom

http://www.twitter.com/grin_com

SHU SHI: Getting Rid Of Loneliness

Reducing loneliness by re-introducing quality communication into lives of independent elderly

Natasha Shroff
University of Amsterdam

ABSTRACT

Independently living elderly are often subject to deep and long-lasting loneliness. With a steadily aging population and a negative population growth rate by 2040, the current problem of lonely elderly is going to increase simultaneously. A smart home-based system was designed to detect loneliness levels and reintroduce quality communication between elderly and their close family members by providing high-level interaction through a multi-modal speech and touch interface including notifications through ambient light panels and a home assistant to let elderly users interact with Shu Shi.

An interactive prototype was created for the course Intelligent Interactive Systems as part of the Information Studies Master at the University of Amsterdam. The system is designed to detect loneliness based on sound sensors, temperature sensors and facial recognition features through the tablet application for the elderly user. Family members can share their mental presence with the elderly in various ways e.g. through sending a commonly shared song to revoke positive memories in the elderly user and reduce the moment of loneliness. There are various types of interpersonal communication such as verbal communication or non-verbal communication i.e. body language, eye contact, facial expression, outward appearance. The system focuses on providing asynchronous communication through various state-of-the-art modalities, designed for to meet the requirements of both elderly and family members.

This report covers the introduction and motivation related to the system, the literature review in related works, followed by the interaction and systems design, discussion and future work sections.

KEYWORDS

Intelligent Interactive Systems, Reducing Loneliness, Ambient Lights, Smart Home, Quality Communication, Speech-to-text, Multi-modal systems

1 INTRODUCTION AND MOTIVATION

Loneliness is a frequently observed phenomenon among independently living single elderly people. With the pension age comes a natural decrease in social relationships since the opportunities to meet new acquaintances is not a part of the daily work life any longer. The loneliness patterns are based on various definitions, i.e. a state of social isolation and identified through low social interaction and a large gap between the current relationships and the desired relationships[20, 33, 48]. We defined loneliness as a feeling of exclusion, feeling of isolation and the tendency towards the absence of friendship.

To decrease the loneliness levels in elderly, certain factors such as quality and frequency of communication with close family members such as children plays an important rule. This type of *asynchronous communication* helps to increase high-quality communication between two different generations. In other words, an older generation that primarily relies on *synchronous communication* e.g. phone calls and a younger generation, busy working long hours and less flexible to answer longer phone calls during the day, therefore prone to using an asynchronous form of communication with their social network through e.g. instant messaging. The contribution of Shu Shi offers an enhanced communication tool for family members to provide ad-hoc emotional and social support to their parents within a few clicks, to bridge the gap between their different communication needs, even throughout a busy workday. The system does not imply that users should avoid synchronous forms of communication with their parents but rather offers a momentary solution to conveniently share their mental presence during the day and ultimately decrease loneliness as well as foster life satisfaction and happiness within the growing segment of elderly while supporting independent living [45, 51, 53].

The solution has three overarching design principles; sustainable by design, privacy by design and inclusion by design. The first principle concerns the green design that the solution promotes e.g. minimize non-renewable energy consumption by aiming to make use of existing hardware in the users' environment such as tablet devices and WiFi speakers that are already part of the users technology assets. Privacy by design incorporates the inherent protection of user data in the design of the solution, e.g. users don't have to configure privacy settings to ensure their data is not shared with third-party providers but the default data privacy is set to the highest privacy level. The third principle inclusion was created to ensure the interaction design includes colors that are appealing to all genders and not is not built gender-specific to begin with, a crucial step towards diversity and inclusion in user design. Another component that also falls under the inclusion category is the diversity in the digital skill range of elderly users, therefore a range from simple interactions with the system to even pro-actively sending over self-recorded material to family members is enabled through the solution.

means plant seed in Chinese and Japanese, it serves as a metaphor for transporting communication gently from one place to another, similar to plant seeds carried by the wind to their next place. Also, seeds are something small than grow into a powerful entity such as a plant, this means that the small seeds of communication that are planted everyday through the system can grow into a strong communication and relationship and eventually overcome loneliness. The system is installed in the home of the elderly and allows convenient communication for both generations through various modalities e.g. speech, touch, light interfaces to facilitate asynchronous, high-level communication with close family members who receive e.g. recorded audio messages from the elderly in transcribed text form on their preferred messenger application and hence contribute to building a closer relationship through increased quality communication. In the related works section, relevant theories to loneliness and communication were identified and analysed for further understanding of the subject matter.

2 RELATED WORK

This section draws on various fields such as psychology, sociology, technology acceptance, use and high-quality communication among elderly.

The causes and consequences of a reduction in social life are explained in detail, leading to a description of loneliness increments and severity levels. Furthermore, asynchronous communication has been defined, followed by the recent developments in user acceptance and technology innovations for elderly to present an overview of currently available industry solutions[1].

2.1 Reduction of Social Life

2.1.1 Causes. From the pension age onward, the social circle of most people starts to reduce naturally since people above the pension-age have less opportunities to make new acquaintances, previously possible through work connections is hence negatively correlated with age[18, 49]. As a side factor, the daily routine drastically changes from a full-time active occupation to a lot of free time and only minor personal administration tasks to manage, hence a rather passive role [7, 52]. However, as research by Adams proposes, elderly do not necessarily have a desire for novelty and meeting new social connections, instead they are looking for creating deeper bonds within existing, reliable relationships [2]. Another reason for the decrease in social activities could be the abandonment by family members and a possible abuse of the helplessness of the elderly as seen in a study in Brazil [52]. The study concluded that loneliness can be seen in different stages of life but is rather prevalent with the elderly age group. Another reason for less contact with family members could be the urbanization and the children moving to bigger cities for higher-paying jobs to support themselves and reach higher levels of self-actualization to satisfy their social needs[39, 42, 51].

2.1.2 Consequences. If those bonds cannot be formed or are not developing in a positive way, the combination with other age-related factors such as decline in physical strength, health, a growing dependency on relatives in terms of financial, physical and mental assistance, the loss of spouses as well as the diminishing economical value can create a level of loneliness that leads to outcomes such as depression, poor sleep quality, anxiety, cognitive decline, circumstances that are difficult to reverse for an individual on their own [2, 19, 25].

According to recent academic research papers, one of the positively related consequences of above-mentioned loneliness levels across age and nationality is depression [50]. In a recent Chinese research study, high levels of loneliness were found to be positively related with high levels of personal dissatisfaction and depression [41]. Often times, individuals would pro-actively distance themselves from their social surroundings while referring their lack of social interaction as the responsibility of other people in their social circle, a social isolation behaviour can lead to depression and physical diseases [13, 59]. Anxiety, a common mental disease is closely related to loneliness and often linked to symptoms such as emotional instability and low social integration [21, 52]. Additional Factors correlated with loneliness among elderly concern poor sleep quality as well as cognitive decline [7, 19].

There are various types of cognitive decline, Mild Cognitive Impairment (MCI), Alzheimer's disease and Dementia were found to be the three most widely occurring phenomena among elderly. MCI is the mildest form of CI and can be categorized in between natural aging effects and the affected elder's beginning stages of dementia, the estimated number of affected elderly above 65 lies between 10-20 percent. Furthermore, it only concerns the cognitive decline, unlike dementia and Alzheimer's which also impair the elder's physical and vocal control abilities [43]. A research conducted by Baumgart suggests that loneliness is linked to cognitive decline through the negative behaviours that it introduces into the elder's life such as a diet high in carbohydrates, trans-fats and sugars, low physical activity and exercise as well as little interaction with regards to cognitive challenge and even alcohol or substance abuse [8]. Consequently, these factors can lead further to poor sleep quality and besides, are all known as contributing factors to cognitive decline[8, 11, 12, 38]. In addition, peer-reviewed research in the field of psychoneuroendocrinology found that loneliness actively increases cortisol levels, a physical state that is linked to cognitive decline through the affection of memory-storing neurons in the brain [23, 54]. Another loneliness-related research finding by a recent study published in the Journals of Gerontology stated that loneliness increases the risk of dementia by 40 percent [55]. A clear link between loneliness and severe consequences of cognitive decline can thus be assumed.

Finally, a previously mentioned association with loneliness was made on the sleep deprivation and poor sleep quality topic. Sleep quality was measured in a Turkish study by Tel, to determine the elder's quality of life. A positive relation between age and poor quality in sleep was found to be significant, as well as a negative relationship between age and life quality, meaning that an increase in age comes with worsened sleep and reduced life quality[56]. An increase in social activities on the other hand, did not result in a better self-recorded sleep quality score on the long-term over a period of five years but rather short-term periods only, according to a recent study by Chen, Lauderdale and Waite[14]. This means that an active social life can be beneficial to good sleep quality and hence less loneliness in elderly, at least on the shorter time-frame[47].

A further consequence of loneliness and the reduction in social life could be personal dissatisfaction among elderly. A recent study by Etxeberria rated the elderly age group on emotional profiles and derived three main categories; the *dissatisfied* with high negative affect, loneliness and unhappiness levels, the *happy* with high levels of life satisfaction and positive affect as well as low levels of loneliness using few passive strategies to regulate emotions and finally the *resilient* with moderate levels of emotional affect and a passive coping strategy [24]. It was noticeably observed that there was a change with the age group of 85 and above mostly classified as resilient, showing higher levels of negative affect than younger participants[16, 24]. Gender categorization and life satisfaction was used in a Korean study, to determine which group would be more inclined to feel lonely, the results showed that the Korean female participants were less susceptible to strong feelings of loneliness because of their natural competence to maintaining close relationships[59]. Overall, it can be concluded that the lack of social relationships, decline in physical and cognitive ability as well as poor sleep quality are positively correlated with loneliness [56].

2.1.3 Countermeasures. Factors that counteract negative long-term outcomes such as depression and anxiety are often traced back to solid social foundations and strong family bonds i.e. frequently visiting children and the attendance of social gatherings i.e. weekly leisure club because of the social and emotional support that such connections provide [14, 15, 21, 32, 41, 50]. Furthermore, a positive relationship between spiritual or religious contributions and a decrease in loneliness was observed by the Brazilian research study, since elderly "were able to cope with the losses imposed by life [...] [by] holding onto a bigger force" [52].

2.2 Levels of Loneliness

Based on the literature review, different levels of loneliness were defined. *Social loneliness* for instance, concerns an individual that is not part of a social group or network any longer, this can take place in the form of a friend group or social gatherings based on similar interests such as spirituality or other leisure activities [20, 41, 52]. A second type is defined as *emotional loneliness*, the lack of a deep emotional bond with another person in ones social environment[20, 41]. This type of emotional bond is not necessarily categorized under romantic relationships but can also take place in close

relationships with friends or relatives, as long as they provide feelings of affection and security.

Weiss' typology concerning social and emotional loneliness defines six social provisions, also known as interpersonal needs [57], including *attachment* and the resulting emotion of safety and security, *social integration* within a network of shared interests, *opportunity for nurturance* to mutually exchange the sense of responsibility, *reassurance of worth* to receive affirmation of ability and skills, *reliable alliance* to foster the security of a reliable social network and finally *guidance* by i.e. receiving advice based on previous life experience [20].

Loneliness can induce a state of emotional instability, lack of self-efficacy, purpose and meaning of the elder's life [8, 26]. These research findings let us to assume that decreasing loneliness can play a significant role in increasing the life quality of elderly.

2.3 Asynchronous Communication

To increase the quality of communication and interaction between the elderly user and the child, certain factors were found to be correlated with good communication should be considered for the system. Since most adult children are busy working during the week and have full schedules with weekend activities to attend to, the strong need for asynchronous and yet effective communication, going beyond than chatting services between elderly and their family members exists[51].

With an aged user group, the different needs in communication need to be accommodated due to a natural decline in physical and cognitive states i.e. hearing or vision impairment. Yorkston found that vocabulary, grammar knowledge and the ability to repeat remain on a similar level, whereas the "comprehension of utterances" is rather inclined to decrease with the age [60].

2.4 Current Technology Assistance Solutions for Elderly

A categorization of technical living-assistance was established by Ruijiao Li and his team to further organize ambient-assisted living (AAL) into daily task facilitation, mobility assistance, healthcare and rehabilitation as well as communication, social inclusion[40]. For above described cognitive decline in the form of Alzheimer's, a number of successfully implemented technologies are available to assist patients through speech-controlled reminder systems who repeatedly play reminders via the speakers or digitally controlled pill-release boxes to help remind patients to take their medicine at the right time of the day[30].

A study by Shen argued that the use of a smart home-care system for elderly would actively extend the amount of time that elderly can live on their own and thus playing an important role in the future of healthcare as a personalized form of health and care assistance[51]. Options for home-care system include the use of smart sensors installed in every room or a television-operated system to ensure the safety surveillance of the elderly user in the own home[27, 51].

2.5 User Technology Acceptance among Elderly

A survey by Pew Research Center collected data from US-American elderly above the age of 65 and found that 30 percent of the target group participants owned a tablet device, 80 percent had a cellphone, 40 percent a smartphone in use[4]. To test the user acceptance of technology among elderly users in the Netherlands, a study was carried out in the case of a home-care system for elderly and stated that elderly had a generally positive attitude towards adapting the system and learning more about different uses. Elements that would contribute to a user acceptance and adaptation are low-cost efficient systems, the sharing of physical instructions cards for the system and benefits to various stakeholders apart from the elderly users [34].

3 INTERACTION DESIGN

The system will be available for elderly tablet users and close family members whom the elderly user would like to interact with on a frequent basis. The tablet is an integral part of the home system, its larger size enables even slightly visually impaired users to make use of the communication service via touch or speech interfaces. It also enables high-level mobility for the user and was deemed suitable for the user group since approximately one third of seniors above 65 already own a tablet based on a 2017 study by Pew Research US [4]. While a smartphone version for the app is a possibility for elderly users who are comfortable using a smartphone or don't own a tablet, this version of the interaction design was directed only towards elderly tablet users due to the large screen size.

3.1 User group persona

Two main user groups were defined to clarify the user needs and requirements within the system, the elderly and the family member. Split into four separate personas, an overview can be found in Table 1.

Persona	Jan	Fiona	Aafke	Anouk
Age	72	77	83	42
Gender	Male	Female	Female	Female
Location	A'dam	Oss	Utrecht	A'dam
Dig. skill	High	Low	Medium	High
Past Job	Techie	Nurse	Teacher	Consult.
Lifestyle	Basic	Basic	Healthy	Stressed
Marital Stat.	Widower	Alone	Alone	Married

Table 1: System User Persona Table

Based on the elderly user personas, a preference for synchronous communication during lonely moments was identified, in contrary to the younger family member who is often restricted to fast-paced, flexible asynchronous communication due to long work hours and full schedules. These two types of communication are not available in current multimodal communication systems such as the FB Messenger

Figure 1: Floor plan with Shu Shi System installed

[1] or the WhatsApp Messenger[2], since they are solely focused on providing either asynchronous communication in the form of messages or synchronous communication through a (video)-call function [58].

3.1.1 Age 72. Jan lives in Amsterdam and is digitally literate. He retired five years ago from his occupation as a technical sales manager and lives in his small but privately owned apartment. He communicates with his children through WhatsApp instant messaging and phone calls, occasionally meets friends in real-life and recently noticed that his children reply less frequent as he desires. Also, he would like to interact with his friend group online but most of them are not willing to download social media apps apart from WhatsApp or Facebook. At home, he uses an iPad to play movies since he connected it via Apple Home to his Smart TV, plays Spotify [3] music via wireless Sonos speakers [4] and reads the daily newspaper *de Volkskrant* as well as various tech innovation magazines on his iPad every morning.

3.1.2 Age 77. Fiona, a long retired nurse from the local hospital longs for more social interaction. In order to find peace from the stressful days that she experienced at work for more than thirty-five years, she has been renting a one-bedroom apartment in the small and quiet town Oss for the past eight years. Fiona highly values her independence of being able to live alone and to decide autonomously about her daily tasks and plans. However, her current social life is based around the caregiver from the weekly social check-up service, the customers that she encounters during her daily grocery shopping trip and the frequent doctoral appointments. Due to her extreme working hours during her former occupation as a nurse, her circle of friends decreased over time down to three loose friendships with ex-colleagues

---

[1] https://www.messenger.com/
[2] https://www.whatsapp.com/
[3] https://www.spotify.com/nl/
[4] https://www.sonos.com/nl-nl/shop/one-sl.html

4

in Oss and a few youth friends in far-away cities, making her feel alone and restless. Her two children visit her about every three months since they work internationally in Germany and Singapore to advance their careers. On her last birthday, Fiona received a tablet as a present from her children. She doesn't use it frequently as she prefers to read newspapers in paper-format and was not given a proper training to make effective use of the device. However, the seclusion and minimal social life build a strong contrast to her previous busy work life, surrounded by patients around the clock. As a result, Fiona felt such deep loneliness and lack of purpose that she was diagnosed with a clinical depression, upon which she decided to take anti-depressants in prior consultation with her long-term psychiatrist. Fiona would actually like to reconnect with her youth friends but is skeptical to make use of technology to reach out to them after so many years of silence.

3.1.3 Age 83. Aafke, a retired teacher lives on her own in the outskirts of Utrecht. She tries to actively engage in communication with others and calls her children and grandchildren on a weekly basis through her landline phone. However, she notices that the phone calls with her family members on average barely last longer than 15 minutes because their weekends are fully scheduled with meetings and plans they already made. Aafke has a few friends from the physiotherapy club that she visits daily. She would like to meet with them more frequently because currently face-to-face meetings outside classes occur only two to three times a month. Aafke is a strong-willed and detail-oriented character which can sometimes lead to slight irritations among her team members. Furthermore, she recently has observed a reoccurring hand tremor and has difficulties controlling the small touch screen applications on her large mobile smartphone. She likes to make use of applications such as Apple Health, WhatsApp and the Safari browser to search for questions that came up in her daily cross-word puzzle in the local newspaper that is delivered to her door every morning. Due to the small font size and limited display area, Aafke quickly reaches exhaustion of the interaction with her smartphone. Aafke thinks that people in her age group rarely show a positive learning attitude towards recent technological innovations, yet she would like to experiment further with home systems to expand her knowledge in this field and meet younger people who are more skilled than her when it comes to technology use.

3.1.4 Age 42. Anouk, daughter of Aafke is the only persona in the family member section because this type of user was found to have similar characteristics in communication needs and lifestyle. She is a highly educated woman with a hard-working attitude to satisfy her own esteem and self-actualization needs e.g. wants to be respected by her colleagues and personal social circles as well as experiencing the need for experimentation and challenging situations respectively. However, because of her full-time consulting job at Accenture in Amsterdam and her two children, she barely has time during the week to even have dinner together with

her family at their house in the nearby Amstelveen. Even though her husband is supports her wherever he can after coming home from his 9 to 5 job at the local municipal office, it is difficult for the family to find some common quality time together. Hence, during the weekends the family spends lots of time doing fun activities together such as attending the hockey tournaments and musical recitals of her children. Besides, Anouk has ambitious hobbies, such as practicing spinning and hot yoga, playing tennis with her friends every Sunday morning. She reads about work-life balance and Zen Buddhism, hires a babysitter every Saturday evening to try different restaurants in town with her husband. She prefers chatting with her friends on WhatsApp and Facebook Messenger to quickly share and get updates about each others weekend activities, listens to audio messages via WhatsApp on the car or bike ride home from work. It would be convenient for her to use a messenger service to communicate with her mother in the short breaks throughout her scheduled day e.g. lunch break, yet still keep her flexibility and send her mother a personal, yet asynchronous message without the text-interface boundaries of WhatsApp and the regular FB Messenger.

3.2 User Group Requirements

Based on the identified personas above, the following user group requirements can be set. Shu Shi was designed for elderly users who live independently, without a partner or direct family members such as Aafke, Jan or Fiona. Elderly users value their independence and the freedom of decision-making in their lives.

To interact with the system in their own home, the elderly users require multi-modal components such as light panels and speakers installed in a frequently visited area of the house to ensure a seamless connection with the audio and notification function of the system. The light panels were chosen as a requirement because the elderly user group can see the notifications immediately based on color scheme to indicate the type of incoming notification and enjoy further benefits of using ambient lights at home. The system needs to adapt to multiple modalities to ensure sufficient flexibility for users such as Aafke who prefer a speech interface over a touch interface.

In order for the ambient light integration to be deployed for notification through light color-schemes, color-blind or severely visually impaired users cannot fully make use of the system yet. To make use of the tablet touchscreen, users should be able to use at least one hand for sufficient device control. Moreover, the elderly user requires a multi-modal access to the system with respect to commanding the system as well as message composition. As far as social relationships extend, a stable relationship between children and the elderly has to exist with room for improvement in terms of high-quality communication, see section 2.3 for further explanation. The user has to be comfortable engaging with a tablet and the speech interface on a daily basis and be willing to share Shu Shi's daily report insights with a family member.

The user group "family member" should be willing to receive multiple push notifications on the smartphone on various occasions throughout the day and use a music streaming service of choice to allow the music integration to be applied within the system.

3.3 Design

Based on the above defined user requirements, the interaction design in Figure 2 was created. There are two interfaces available to the elderly user, consisting of the tablet application via touch control and the speech interface that is connected to the home assistant e.g. Siri and the Apple Homekit [6]. Family members can make use of the system through various messenger applications such as Facebook Messenger or Rocket.Chat[5].

Various heuristics as defined by Nielsen [44, 46] are vital to the interaction design such as the visibility of system status i.e. informing users of the current state and processes running within the application. Besides, there has to be a match between the system and the real world i.e. a metaphor used to describe the connection between the system to adapt to users' needs such as a particular language, words and phrases and other components that the user already knows [35]. For instance, within the Shu Shi system, the tablet interface is adjustable in font size, see Figure 3e, to enable even the slightly visually impaired user to comfortably read the color-scheme categorization for the notification through the light panels and see images clearly as visualized in Figure 3h.

Another heuristic element is the user control and freedom to enable the user to exit and interact with the application at any point in time, consistency and standards as well as flexibility and efficiency of use are directly applicable to the interaction design. Help and documentation, another heuristic is available in the form of the button that links the user to the color scheme of lights to understand the differences in colors and light patterns, displayed by the integrated Nanoleaf subsystem [44, 46].

3.3.1 Initial Set-up. The Shu Shi application has to be downloaded in the Apple Store[6] for iOS users and the Play Store [7] for Android users, the interfaces created in this section only include the iOS designed due to time and space constraints. For a successful user registration, an initial set-up has to be completed on the tablet application, or if not otherwise possible e.g. assistance required, through the mobile phone application of the family member. An initial questionnaire as visualized in Figure 3a is part of the set-up to understand the user situation in terms of entering personal data and adding family members in Figure 3b, configuring settings for the ambient light notifications in Figure 3c and register hardware for integration with Shu Shi in Figure 3d.

Music genre preferences are also included to enable the music recommendations, sent from family members to elderly users. If the user wants to adjust e.g. privacy settings further as visualized in Figure 3e, general settings are accessible from the home screen through the setting button in the lower right corner of the footer menu.

The system knows to propose which interface by location detection i.e. it requires to know the location by for instance, using infrared sensors to locate the elder through body heat detection. During the initial set-up phase, the options for the interface per room have to also be identified by the user e.g. speakers and Nanoleaf available in each room or just one room, see Figure 1 for a floor plan of the installed system.

3.3.2 Interaction Phase. Upon completion of the setup phase, a daily questionnaire called "FeelWell Session" has to be filled in by the elderly to inquire the user's loneliness state through either voice or touch such as Figure 3g shows.

The daily FeelWell Session reminder is prompted on the Nanoleaf light panels with a green light as visible in Figure 2. The questions are adapted from the UCLA loneliness scale [8] and are prompted to the user in variations to avoid user response manipulation bias. The measurement scale was adjusted from the original four-point Likert scale consisting of the following levels of agreements: never, rarely, sometimes, often. The new scale consists of: satisfied, a little satisfied, a little dissatisfied and dissatisfied, to indicate the users satisfaction levels as previous literature research findings showed that personal dissatisfaction is positively related to loneliness levels in section 2.1.2.

3.4 Ambient light notifications

The arrival of an interpersonal message from the child to the parent is communicated by a channel device that gives off colored light-signals to signify the arrival of a new message to the receiver. A Japanese study on the effects on emotions by being dazzled with colored light found that light-blue color alerts the user slightly more than other colors used in the study, which is why the color blue is suggested as the default notification color for incoming messages to gently, yet effectively catch the attention of the elderly user [31]. To allow users to freely select their preferred notification color, green and purple are given as additional options. The purple color is ranked lower than blue and green regarding the user's attention according to Ehlers and was hence suggested as a color for system notifications such as required updates, privacy consent agreements or other system push notifications requiring action taken by the user [22].

Since the color green is found to be related to happiness, calmness and serenity, it was chosen as the default notification color to remind the elderly user to complete the daily FeelWell session[28].

---

[5] https://Rocket.Chat/
[6] https://www.apple.com/
[7] https://play.google.com/store

[8] https://sparqtools.org/mobility-measure/ucla-loneliness-scale-version-3/

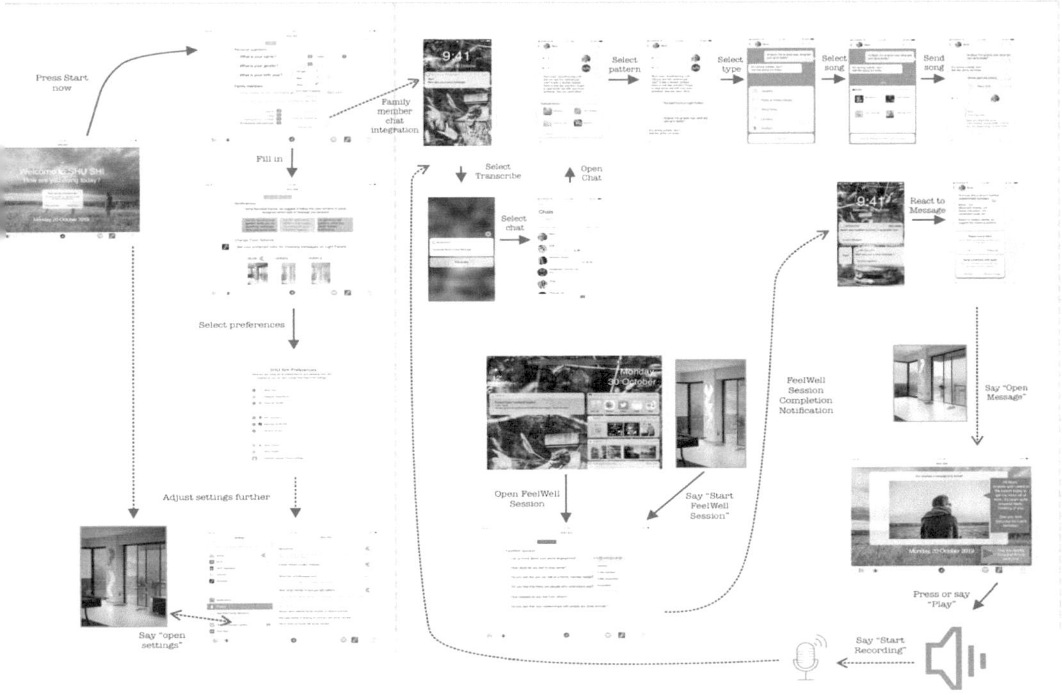

Figure 2: Interaction Design Overview.

(a) Setup Screen Tablet

(b) Initial Setup Personal Info

(c) Initial Setup Color Scheme

(d) Initial Setup Settings

(e) General Settings

(f) FeelWell Tablet Notification

(g) FeelWell Session

(h) Tablet Image Message

Figure 3: User Interfaces for Elderly User on Tablet

(a) Messenger Contacts   (b) Choose Light Pattern   (c) Light Pattern Sent   (d) Choose Message Type

(e) Choose Song   (f) Song Sent   (g) Open Summary   (h) Choose Message Options

Figure 4: User Interfaces for Family Member on Smartphone.

3.5 Voice Control

To enable the user to interact with the speech interface of the system, the microphone has to be adjusted in the privacy settings visualized in Figure 3e. The voice control is managed through the home assistant such as Google Home or Apple's Siri. For instance, a family member sent a song to the elderly, see Figure 4d,e,f for clarification. If the elderly user plays this song, the play prompt can be addressed to the system via speech such as "Siri, open message". If the

elderly user then decides to reply back to the family member, both speech and text modalities can be used to send the message as visualized in Figure 4b on the upper part of the interface in the form of an audio message or a simple text message if otherwise preferred by the elderly user. To exemplify user empowerment, the elderly user can use the system for pro-active communication with family members, i.e. the communication works both ways and does not need a trigger from the family member to allow for communication between the two parties. The contact button is also included in the lower footer menu of the Shu Shi tablet application, to allow the user to see and reach out to the contacts in a convenient manner, see Figure 3a for more information.

3.6 Messenger Chat Modality: Family Members

The messenger chat includes the elderly user as a regular contact as visualized in Figure 4a. Family members can select a Nanoleaf light panel patterns based on four templates or create their own color pattern with the Nanoleaf API [9]. The elderly user can decide to allow or restrict Nanoleaf patterns to be displayed that are sent by family members in the general settings in Figure3e.

3.6.1 Speech to Text Transcription Modality. To enable the wishes of the family member user group for efficient asynchronous communication via text, a speech to text function was integrated into the messenger interface. if there is little time during the day, users can easily let the system transcribe voice messages to text as visualized in Figure4b and c. While listening to personal voice messages enables the message receiver to detect emotions through the voice of the message sender, the transcription is meant for busy situations in which the family member is still able to reply quickly and take action if required based on the emotions detected in the transcription. A summary of the FeelWell session reported by the elderly will be sent to the family member in text form, as visualized in Figure4h with two possibilities to send the elderly user either a memory or even skip the asynchronous communication for a real-time call or video chat in case of severe loneliness levels. This decision-making process is handed over to the family members' authority to support autonomous decision-making.

4 SYSTEMS DESIGN

The systems design section consists of an explanation regarding the internal structure of the system, including a systems architecture visualization in Figure 5 as well as the requirements, input and output of the system.

The open intelligent interactive system was designed to facilitate high-quality communication between elderly and close family members to ultimately decrease the emotional distance between the two users and consists of a multi-modal speech to text interface with face and voice recognition.

4.1 Hardware Components

In order to use Shu Shi, several hardware components are required to make full use of the system's capabilities. The elderly user requires a tablet comparable to a device running on iOS 11.0 or Android tablet 6.0 and later versions[29] and one frontal camera with a >1.2-megapixel resolution[5], required for recording clear video messages or photos e.g. addressed to family members. Current market-leading tablet devices provide a storage capacity of either 32GB or 128GB,

of which the latter is recommended for immediate retrieval and offline access to all user media data stored within the application [5]. The actual required working memory depends on the amount of devices and users registered in the system as well as the type and amount of messages exchanged between users. All message data such as images or videos are stored on the tablet itself as well as in the local cloud called "Shu Shi Server" as visualized in Figure5. The device also includes an in-built microphone and speaker to record audio messages and videos with audio files for enhanced communication between Shu Shi users.

An additional extension of the tablet in-built audio functions would be a smart WiFi speaker subsystem such as Sonos One[10], allowing for streaming of services such as Spotify, Apple Music, Napster[11] Google Play Music[12] via Google Home, Apple's HomeKit or Amazon's Alexa assistant[13]. Furthermore, the elderly user have to install a minimum of one Nanoleaf Aurora light panel[14] to receive message notifications, system notifications as well as light patterns sent from family members, as previously explained in the ambient light notifications section and seen in Figure 2. The Nanoleaf light panel starter kit with three light panels is included during the first system purchase as it is a critical system component to notify the user of incoming messages in a subtle way without the tablet as an additional interaction medium barrier and possible distraction to the elderly user. Furthermore, the ambient lights can be easily integrated with an assistant such as Homekit, Alexa and Google Home, which also builds an integral part of the system. According to Nanoleaf.me, the user can create a more natural daylight setting and change the atmosphere of the room through the light panels, which is ideal for the Shu Shi system, since the elderly users can create a more homely or comfortable sphere through the ambient lights, while being notified of messages immediately. Ideally, one Nanoleaf light panel is installed in every room of the elder's home for extended reach of the system to the user, for instance, if the elderly is located in a separate kitchen, the notification light can be redirected to the kitchen, as visualized in the floor plan in Figure 1.

To enable the in-home locating user function, a passive infrared (PIR) sensor is required for body heat detection based on changing levels of body heat within different grid zones. The infrared sensor is not part of the initial system purchase set but can be rather seen as an additional system extension tool since the small detection range would require various infrared sensors, which would increase the system price by around 40 USD[15] and are not required for the system to provide its basic functionalities to the user. The infrared sensor

---

[9]https://nanoleaf.me/en/consumer-led-lighting/products/smarter-series/nanoleaf-cloud/nanoleaf-local-api/

[10]https://www.sonos.com/nl-nl/shop/one.html
[11]https://us.napster.com/
[12]https://play.google.com/store/music?hl=en
[13]https://apps.apple.com/us/app/amazon-alexa/id944011620
[14]https://nanoleaf.me/en/consumer-led-lighting/products/smarter-series/nanoleaf-light-panels-smarter-kit/
[15]https://www2.meethue.com/en-us/p/hue-motion-sensor/046677473389

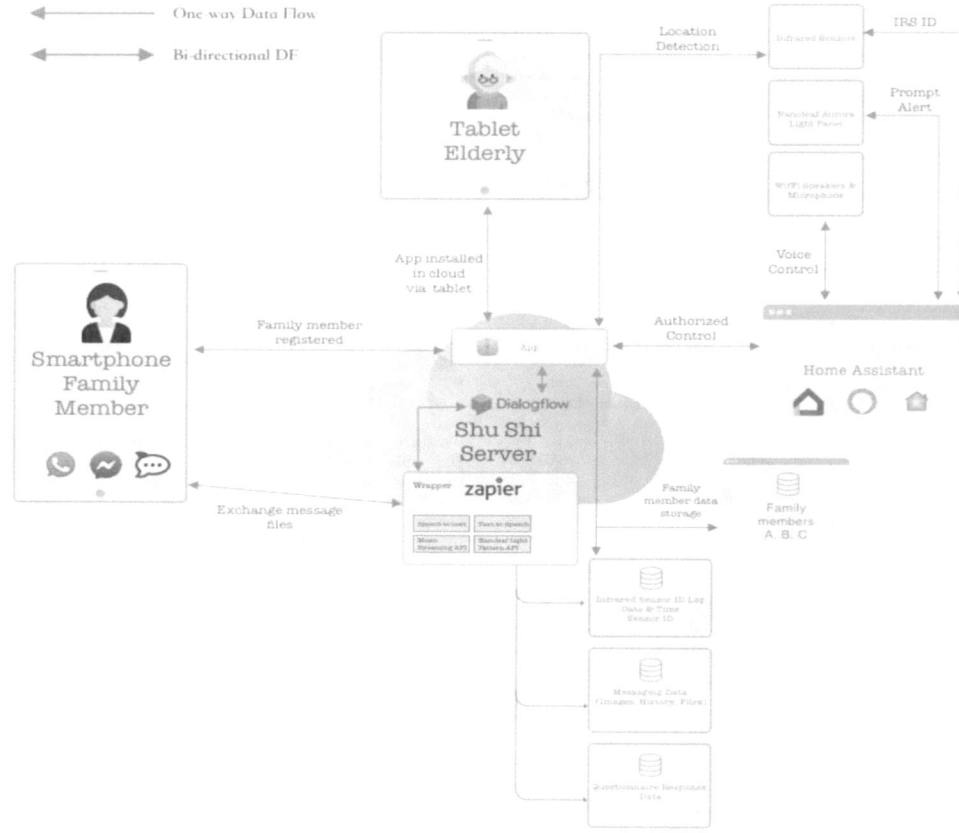

Figure 5: System Design Visualization.

Common smart PIR devices such as 1byone's PIR sensor[16] have a detection range of 5-8m and therefore has to be installed in every room.

The participating family members require a smart, mobile device with an OS comparable to iOS 8.0, Android 4.0 and above[17], capable of running a bot-integrated messenger application such as Rocket.Chat or Facebook messenger, it has to have a 2GB RAM memory [10] to run the messenger application. A front and/or back camera is suggested optimal use of the communication exchange service.

4.2 Software Components

This section describes the software elements of the system by providing an explanation for each user action and identifies the system responses through data input and output for both user groups, the elderly and family members. A system architecture was created to clarify the various components required for the system to work and is visualized in Fig 5.

[16]https://1byone.com/wireless-home-security-driveway-alarm-2-sensor-1-receiver-adapter.html

[17]https://www.facebook.com/help/messenger-app/197039404112757

?rared Sensor: ID	Message: Type	Daily Questionnaire
IS_ID	Message_Date	ID_Questionnaire
?om_ID	Sender_Name	Time_Questionnaire
?S_Time	Content_Text	Loneliness_Score
		Score_Suggestion

Figure 6: Database tables.

4.2.1 Data model.
This section describes the data model of the Shu Shi system, based on Figure 5 and the database tables in Figure 6. Several types of data are generated by the elderly users. Stored in the Shu Shi Server, they are captured through the application and sensors. The elderly users generate location data by moving through the home and passing by light barriers radiated from the various infrared sensors, which are then assigned an individual ID and time stamp to identify the approximate location of the user for automatic light panel notifications in the right location of the home. In addition, the elderly users generate quantitative personal data during the daily questionnaire, which results in a loneliness score based on the UCLA loneliness scale questions rated by the elder. The third data generation source are the messages that are sent between elderly and family members including text, audio, video and light pattern formats. To run a messenger application that allows for bot-integration such as Rocket.Chat or Facebook Messenger, the family member has to install one of those messenger applications.

The data labels for the user data are identified in Figure 6. An additional database was created for the family members as part of Figure 5 because the data about the available messenger chat application of the family member has to be stored in the Shu Shi Server as it is processed through the application integration tool Zapier[18] to convert an audio message sent by the elderly into text.

4.2.2 System Processes: Elderly.
During the *setup phase* in which the users answer the initial questionnaire to i.a. enter the available and installed hardware of the elderly user, the first user input is processed. Elderly users enter personal data such as UserName, UserGender, UserAge and the registration of the family members whom they desire a closer connection with, consequently stored in the family member database as explained in the data model section. The setup also requires the user to setup the available hardware and, upon physical installation, connect it to the system through the tablet application.

After the setup is completed, the users move on to the active phase of user communication through the system. The first user action process is the natural *movement and location* through the home. Hereby, the data input source are several infrared sensors. The infrared sensors determine the body heat level of the user and thus deliver input to locate the user within the home through a Sensor ID coming from the home assistant. The function of the sensors is to constantly match if the Sensor ID has changed and if that is the case thereby retrieving the users location within the home. The data is stored in the Sensor ID database table as visualized in Figure 6 that covers the relation between the room and sensor IDs in the Shu Shi Server, seen in Figure 5. The data output of the infrared sensors is the current user location in terms of room ID and to provide the application with the available presentation modes e.g. the nearest light panel to prompt notifications.

The second data generation process in the active user phase of the elderly group is to conduct the *daily questionnaire*. Generation of data occurs by responding to the daily questions during the FeelWell session for the elderly user and is captured either through the WiFi speakers who are connected to the home assistant, processed by Google's DialogFlow API[19]. The data output of the daily questionnaire is the loneliness score which is then transformed into a small scorecard report and, upon given consent of the elderly user in the privacy settings, sent to the family members messenger chat as an output. This loneliness score report will trigger a suggestion to the family member to take a small action upon receiving the summary such as Thirdly, the *audio messages* generated by the elderly can be transformed into text, using the Google Speech to Text API[20] as part of the Zapier automation tool in Figure 5 since the family member target group prefers text as a convenient format to quickly read and respond to messages, as previously explained in the related works and interaction design user persona sections.

4.2.3 System Processes: Family Members.
The family member has just one input source, namely the third-party messenger application with its various message formats apart from text format. The user action process can be described as *Interaction Process with Elderly*. Besides regular text format, several other data formats are available that can be shared through the messenger with the elderly. Images, videos, audio messages are already part of the standard messenger function. To create more diversity, Nanoleaf light patterns are available to signify emotions or moods to the elderly and suggest a particular ambient atmosphere in the elder's home. The light pattern can be either developed by the family member through the Nanoleaf website and then imported into the messenger light pattern library or chosen from the existing Nanoleaf light pattern library that is integrated in the messenger application as a plug-in. Similarly, songs can be shared through third-party music streaming services images, videos to share common memories. As a third alternative format, a "memory" format was created to combine a photo or video file with a newly recorded "voice-over" audio file, see Figure 4h for a visualization. The family member can send this memory format after receiving the daily questionnaire summary in the messenger application.

---

[18]https://zapier.com/

[19]https://dialogflow.com/
[20]https://cloud.google.com/text-to-speech/

The internal system processes the input from the smartphone and tablet modalities as well as the various additional input sources specified in the modalities layer. To process the input, several API's are used in the back-end layer of the system such as the Google Cloud Speech API i.e. audio message transcribes audio message to Google Home which then sends the audio data to the bot-integrated in the messenger. External API's such as the speech-to-text cloud API, the text-to-speech cloud API are also connected to the system through automation tool Zapier in the Shu Shi server.

The system output of the family member's interaction with the elderly is communicated via the Shu Shi Server to multiple output sources such as the WiFi speakers for songs and audio messages, the tablet for visualizing images, videos and memories, the Nanoleaf light panels for showing light patterns or notification signals. The Shu Shi server handles all calculations and database updates, as well as the connection with the family members. The home assistant serves to handle the communication with the elderly, the respective API is communicating with the Shu Shi application and the Shu Shi server database to fetch the required data e.g. notification prompts for light patterns to displayed.

5   DISCUSSION

During the project, the system design was reiterated various times and a discussion on various system functions and integration was held frequently to answer the research theme "decreasing loneliness levels in elderly". One of the first major changes in the user flexibility of the system design was related to the exchange of messages between the elderly and the family members. While the project group first thought of constraining the elderly user by only allowing a passive reply function to messages from family members, the system was then redesigned to allow for a free-flowing exchange of communication between the users to give flexibility and freedom to the elder since the elderly user requirements underline the importance of independence and decision-making authority.

5.1   System Diversity

In the beginning stages, the system was only meant for Facebook messenger users since the age group of 30-45 year old's was found to be a frequent user of the messenger [17]. To diversify the user group and allow various messenger applications to be used for user convenience as well as to lower the threshold for the user to make use of the system, multiple messengers such as Rocket.Chat were included in the design for system integration options. Additional integration for messengers such as Line [21], Telegram[22] or WeChat[23] should be discussed further to increase user-friendliness.

The system currently does not inform the family member if a message has been opened by the elderly through either the tablet or via voice control. To improve the safety measure functionalities for elderly within the system, the data

could be communicated back to the family member in the form of a grey and blue check mark, similar to the message delivered and read check mark categorization in messenger chat applications such as WhatsApp[24].

5.2   Heuristics

Related to the usability of a system is the *mobility aspect*. Mobility of the elderly user at home was a point of frequent reiteration to allow the elderly user to interact with the speech interface in all areas of the home. The first version of the interaction design required a fixed station for an iPad, taking away all means of mobility for the elderly user by forcing the user to return to the station for the daily questionnaire and reporting back to the system through the tablet's microphone and camera, initially also allowing facial recognition to support the emotional detection of loneliness, a concept that was then adapted into the current tablet modality to increase feasibility among the user group and to encourage movement within or even outside the home. In case of an expansion outside the home, a smartphone version of the tablet application would be required to implement the increased mobility function. A side effect of the smartphone version could be an increase in elderly system users since 40 percent of the elderly taking part in a digital asset study in the US already owned smartphones [4].

5.2.1   *User authority.* This section addresses the authority and decision-making freedom of the elderly. As of now, the system restricts the elderly to audio messages as the sole outgoing message type that can be sent to the family member. This communication constraint holds back elderly from supporting autonomous decision-making processes and their advancement in digital literacy since only one type of message format can be used. While the elderly user requirements suggest an intermediate digital literacy, the system should encourage users to learn more about the various forms of communication available to e.g. the family members, whose user requirements were classified with a high digital literacy.

5.3   Sensor limitations

The infrared sensors installed in the elder's home serve to detect the user location and generate location data to let the nearest ambient light prompt notifications. However, the infrared light only covers a span of 5-8m to detect objects that let the light reflect back on the sensor and furthermore, send off light rays in a v-shape, hereby creating blind spots that have to be accounted for to properly locate the user. The system requirements specify one PIR sensor per room. The interaction design chapter includes a room plan for a single-room studio with three infrared sensors installed on the walls. Given the elderly user lives in a multi-bedroom apartment, this would only work if they are installed beside the entrance of each room to serve as a laser barrier sensor due to the limited reach of the light as described above. To install the infrared sensors in such a position, users have to

---

[21]https://line.me/en/
[22]https://telegram.org/
[23]https://web.wechat.com/

[24]https://faq.whatsapp.com/en/android/28000015/

either place the sensor on a piece of furniture directly located next to the door frame, or manually install the sensor onto a near wall for a stable device position. This type of installation barrier could possibly hinder the elderly user from fully integrating the system into the home. To further convenience the elderly user group, the system should either provide a sensor that can easily be installed with e.g. double-sided tape or as an alternative, provide multiple room schemes for common apartment layouts among the target group for optimal use of the infrared sensors and increase customer service scalability by providing diverse room schemes in the Shu Shi application.

Another point of discussion is the emotional sensor-based recognition which has not been implemented in the current system. The idea is to record, analyze and evaluate the facial expressions of the elderly on an ongoing basis via external cameras installed in the living room or through the tablet camera to provide a more accurate and data-based prediction on the emotional state and loneliness level of the elderly. With a data-based loneliness prediction, the answers on the daily FeelWell questionnaire could be supported and even compared for any divergence in loneliness ratings. A public benefit from gathering such large amounts of data would be the increased advancement of current facial recognition technologies such as Microsoft's Face API[25]. The increase in training data to feed the machine learning algorithm over time could result in a reduction of social and personal bias generated by the individual programmer and reduce error rates of e.g. classification algorithms. However, the *data privacy* of elderly users could potentially be reduced, since the data would have to be processed on external third-party servers which makes it challenging to track the use and implementation of such personal data. To highlight various ethical standpoints to this argument, a perspective mounting from consequentialism would argue for the greatest good for the greatest number of people, e.g. the benefits for the majority of technology users who would make use of facial recognition to achieve various personal, social or institutional goals and thus would support the installment of additional cameras in the elder's home [9]. However, a deontological perspective such as Kant's categorical imperative calls for the moral duty of integrity and preservation for individual dignity of humans in which the use of personal data would not be supported as all human beings ought to be treated with respect and given moral autonomy [3, 36].

6 CONCLUSION AND FUTURE WORK

The three design principles; sustainable by design, privacy by design and inclusion by design were followed while creating the system. For instance, by encouraging the use of existing devices, protecting the user privacy with privacy sharing settings, and aiming to increase the digital literacy of elderly users through Shu Shi's user-friendly tablet interface. Shu Shi system shows that it enables high quality asynchronous

communication between elderly users and their close family members can be established through a multi-modal intelligent interactive system.

It can be argued that it decreases loneliness levels of elderly as it provides an efficient system for reminding and allowing users to interact with each other, in particular reminding the family member to e.g. send a thoughtful message to the elder based on a daily loneliness questionnaire reported to the system by the elder. The Nanoleaf light panels introduce an alternative method of notifying the elderly user of incoming messages and thus even more so facilitating the elderly to communicate according to their previously specified communication needs and abilities based on an adaptive multi-modality approach. In the previous section, issues and challenges during the research have been discussed, followed by several future work aspects such as *loneliness detection* and *mobility* explained in the following paragraphs.

We suggest to expand the communication options for elderly to other social groups such as friend or hobby groups to diversify the spectrum of interactions and enrich the elder's opportunities to communicate with connections in a similar age group or with similar interests. In terms of diversification, the user interfaces have only been designed for Apple devices so far, a further development for various other operating systems and devices would be desirable since time constraints limited the design to one type of operating system. However, various sections such as hardware requirements include specifications for e.g. both Apple and Android operating systems.

Since the current version of the system does not allow emotion or user movement detection through e.g. facial recognition or temperature sensors, future work is suggested to move into the direction of improving the loneliness detection function. Shu Shi is i.a. meant for reducing social loneliness which was found to be negatively related to physical and leisure activity. Yet, the mobility scope is limited to the home of the elderly user, it would therefore be useful to expand the system into a mobile application for smartphone users as previously discussed and allow elderly to share messages even outside their home, especially since loneliness is often related to low social activity and social isolation of elderly[37, 41, 48].

Finally, a user-friendly function that was not included in the system due to time constraints was a song recommendation system for the family member messenger. Instead of family members sending their own chosen songs to the elderly, an additional preferred genre and song component could be added to the initial setup for the elderly to encourage the exchange of preferred music titles between family members and the elderly. In summary, there are various research possibilities to further improve the loneliness of elderly, especially in regards to the system's mobility expansion and early loneliness detection and prevention.

REFERENCES

[1] All articles in this reference list were accessed on October 25 2019 Above. [n. d.]. All articles in this reference list were accessed

---

[25]https://azure.microsoft.com/en-au/services/cognitive-services/face/

13

online. ([n. d.]).

[2] K B Adams, S Sanders, and E A Auth. 2004. Loneliness and depression in independent living retirement communities: risk and resilience factors. *Aging & Mental Health* 8, 6 (nov 2004), 475–485. https://doi.org/10.1080/13607860410001725054

[3] Anita L. Allen. 2016. Protecting One's Own Privacy in a Big Data Economy - Harvard Law Review. (2016). https://harvardlawreview.org/2016/12/protecting-ones-own-privacy-in-a-big-data-economy/

[4] Monica Anderson, Andrew Perrin, and Aaron Smith. 2017. *FOR MEDIA OR OTHER INQUIRIES*. Technical Report. www.pewresearch.org.

[5] Apple. 2019. iPad 10.2-inch - Technical Specifications - Apple. (2019). https://www.apple.com/ipad-10.2/specs/

[6] Apple. 2019. Siri - Apple Developer. (2019). https://developer.apple.com/siri/

[7] Rukuye Aylaz, Ümmühan Aktürk, Behice Erci, Hatice Öztürk, and Hakime Aslan. 2012. Relationship between depression and loneliness in elderly and examination of influential factors. *Archives of Gerontology and Geriatrics* 55, 3 (nov 2012), 548–554. https://doi.org/10.1016/J.ARCHGER.2012.03.006

[8] Matthew Baumgart, Heather M. Snyder, Maria C. Carrillo, Sam Fazio, Hye Kim, and Harry Johns. 2015. Summary of the evidence on modifiable risk factors for cognitive decline and dementia: A population-based perspective. *Alzheimer's & Dementia* 11, 6 (jun 2015), 718–726. https://doi.org/10.1016/j.jalz.2015.05.016

[9] Leslie Becker. 2012. Design and Ethics: Sealed-off Thinking. *interactions* 19, 2 (mar 2012), 51–53. https://doi.org/10.1145/2090150.2090163

[10] Dennis Bednarz. 2016. Minimum RAM requirement Messenger. (2016). https://www.onmsft.com/news/minimum-ram-requirement-for-facebook-and-messenger-now-up-to-2gb

[11] Lisa F Berkman, Thomas Glass, Ian Brissette, and Teresa E Seeman. 2000. From social integration to health: Durkheim in the new millennium. *Social science & medicine* 51, 6 (2000), 843–857.

[12] Lisa F Berkman, Thomas Glass, Ian Brissette, and Teresa E Seeman. 2000. From social integration to health: Durkheim in the new millennium This paper is adapted from Berkman, L.F., & Glass, T. Social integration, social networks, social support and health. In L. F. Berkman & I. Kawachi, Social Epidemiology. New York: Oxfor. *Social Science & Medicine* 51, 6 (2000), 843–857. https://doi.org/10.1016/S0277-9536(00)00065-4

[13] John T. Cacioppo, Louise C. Hawkley, Gary G. Berntson, John M. Ernst, Amber C. Gibbs, Robert Stickgold, and J. Allan Hobson. 2002. Do Lonely Days Invade the Nights? Potential Social Modulation of Sleep Efficiency. *Psychological Science* 13, 4 (jul 2002), 384–387. https://doi.org/10.1111/1467-9280.00469

[14] Jen-Hao Chen, Diane S Lauderdale, and Linda J Waite. 2016. Social participation and older adults' sleep. *Social science & medicine (1982)* 149 (jan 2016), 164–73. https://doi.org/10.1016/j.socscimed.2015.11.045

[15] Jen-Hao Chen, Linda J. Waite, and Diane S. Lauderdale. 2015. Marriage, Relationship Quality, and Sleep among U.S. Older Adults. *Journal of Health and Social Behavior* 56, 3 (sep 2015), 356–377. https://doi.org/10.1177/0022146515594631

[16] Jinmyoung Cho, Peter Martin, and Leonard W Poon. 2013. Age Group Differences in Positive and Negative Affect among Oldest-Old Adults: Findings from the Georgia Centenarian Study. *The International Journal of Aging and Human Development* 77, 4 (nov 2013), 261–288. https://doi.org/10.2190/AG.77.4.a

[17] J. Clement. 2018. U.S. Facebook Messenger reach by age 2018 | Statista. (2018). https://www.statista.com/statistics/814100/share-of-us-internet-users-who-use-facebook-messenger-by-age/

[18] Benjamin Cornwell, Edward O. Laumann, and L. Philip Schumm. 2008. The Social Connectedness of Older Adults: A National Profile. *American Sociological Review* 73, 2 (apr 2008), 185–203. https://doi.org/10.1177/000312240807300201

[19] M.D. Costa, H. Espírito-Santo, S.C. Simões, C.R. Correia, R. Almeida, L. Ferreira, Á. Conde, V. Alves, F. Ferreira, L. Caldas, I.T. Pena, A. Costa, D. Simões, F. Daniel, and L. Lemos. 2013. 1549 Correlates of elderly loneliness. *European Psychiatry* 28 (jan 2013), 1. https://doi.org/10.1016/S0924-9338(13)76559-3

[20] Enrico DiTommaso and Barry Spinner. 1997. Social and emotional loneliness: A re-examination of weiss' typology of loneliness. *Personality and Individual Differences* 22, 3 (mar 1997), 417–427. https://doi.org/10.1016/S0191-8869(96)00204-8

[21] Joan Domènech-Abella, Jordi Mundó, Josep Maria Haro, and Maria Rubio-Valera. 2019. Anxiety, depression, loneliness and social network in the elderly: Longitudinal associations from The Irish Longitudinal Study on Ageing (TILDA). *Journal of Affective Disorders* (2019). https://doi.org/10.1016/j.jad.2018.12.043

[22] Hans Jürgen Ehlers. 1985. The use of colour to help visualize information. *Computers & Graphics* 9, 2 (1985), 171–176. https://doi.org/10.1016/0097-8493(85)90027-5

[23] Elissa Epel. 2009. Psychological and metabolic stress: A recipe for accelerated cellular aging? *Hormones* 8, 1 (2009), 7–22. https://doi.org/10.14310/horm.2002.1217

[24] Igone Etxeberria, Itziar Etxebarria, and Elena Urdaneta. 2018. Profiles in emotional aging: does age matter? *Aging & Mental Health* 22, 10 (oct 2018), 1304–1312. https://doi.org/10.1080/13607863.2017.1286450

[25] Franziska Förster, Alexander Pabst, Janine Stein, Susanne Röhr, Margrit Löbner, Kathrin Heser, Lisa Miebach, Anne Stark, André Hajek, Birgitt Wiese, Wolfgang Maier, Matthias C. Angermeyer, Martin Scherer, Michael Wagner, Hans Helmut König, and Steffi G. Riedel-Heller. 2019. Are older men more vulnerable to depression than women after losing their spouse? Evidence from three German old-age cohorts (AgeDifferent.de platform). *Journal of Affective Disorders* 256 (sep 2019), 650–657. https://doi.org/10.1016/j.jad.2019.06.047

[26] Laura Fratiglioni, Stephanie Paillard-Borg, and Bengt Winblad. 2004. An active and socially integrated lifestyle in late life might protect against dementia. *The Lancet Neurology* 3, 6 (2004), 343–353. https://doi.org/10.1016/S1474-4422(04)00767-7

[27] A Gaddam, S C Mukhopadhyay, and G S Gupta. 2010. Towards the Development of a Cognitive Sensors Network Based Home for Elder Care. In *2010 6th International Conference on Wireless and Mobile Communications*. 484–491. https://doi.org/10.1109/ICWMC.2010.93

[28] Sandrine Gil and Ludovic Le Bigot. 2014. Seeing life through positive-tinted glasses: color-meaning associations. *PLoS ONE* 9, 8 (2014), e104291. https://doi.org/10.1371/journal.pone.0104291

[29] Google. 2019. Google Nest device specifications - Google Nest Help. (2019). https://support.google.com/googlenest/answer/7072284?hl=en

[30] Kelly Anne Grindrod, Melissa Li, and Allison Gates. 2014. Evaluating user perceptions of mobile medication management applications with older adults: a usability study. *JMIR mHealth and uHealth* 2, 1 (2014), e11. https://doi.org/10.2196/mhealth.3048

[31] Mitsuhiko Hanada. 2015. Effects of Colors on the Feeling of Being Dazzled Evoked by Stimuli with Luminance Gradients. *Perceptual and Motor Skills* 121, 1 (2015), 219–232. https://doi.org/10.2466/27.29.PMS.121c12x8

[32] Floor Holvast, Huibert Burger, Margot M.W. De Waal, Harm W.J. Van Marwijk, Hannie C. Comijs, and Peter F.M. Verhaak. 2015. Loneliness is associated with poor prognosis in late-life depression: Longitudinal analysis of the Netherlands study of depression in older persons. *Journal of Affective Disorders* (2015). https://doi.org/10.1016/j.jad.2015.06.036

[33] Mary Elizabeth Hughes, Linda J. Waite, Louise C. Hawkley, and John T. Cacioppo. 2004. A Short Scale for Measuring Loneliness in Large Surveys. *Research on Aging* 26, 6 (nov 2004), 655–672. https://doi.org/10.1177/0164027504268574

[34] Pengxiang Jia, Yuan Lu, and Barbara Wajda. 2015. Designing for Technology Acceptance in an Ageing Society through Multi-stakeholder Collaboration. *Procedia Manufacturing* 3 (2015), 3535–3542. https://doi.org/10.1016/j.promfg.2015.07.701

[35] Anna Kaley. 2018. Match Between System and Real World: 2nd Usability Heuristic Explained. (2018). https://www.nngroup.com/articles/match-system-real-world/

[36] IMMANUEL Kant, J B Schneewind, Marcia Baron, and Shelly Kagan. 2002. *Groundwork for the Metaphysics of Morals*. Yale University Press. http://www.jstor.org/stable/j.ctt1njjwt

[37] Eric Klinenberg. 2016. Social Isolation, Loneliness, and Living Alone: Identifying the Risks for Public Health. *American Journal of Public Health* 106, 5 (may 2016), 786–787. https://doi.org/10.2105/AJPH.2016.303166

[38] Dexia Kong, Joan Davitt, and XinQi Dong. 2018. Loneliness, Depressive Symptoms, and Cognitive Functioning Among U.S. Chinese Older Adults. *Gerontology & geriatric medicine* 4 (jul 2018), 2333721418778201–2333721418778201. https://doi.org/10.1177/2333721418778201

14

[39] David Lester. 2013. Measuring Maslow's Hierarchy of Needs. *Psychological Reports* 113, 1 (aug 2013), 15–17. https://doi.org/10.2466/02.20.PR0.113x16z1

[40] Ruijiao Li, Bowen Lu, and Klaus D McDonald-Maier. 2015. Cognitive assisted living ambient system: a survey. *Digital Communications and Networks* 1, 4 (2015), 229–252. https://doi.org/10.1016/j.dcan.2015.10.003

[41] Lijun Liu, Zhenggang Gou, and Junnan Zuo. 2016. Social support mediates loneliness and depression in elderly people. *Journal of Health Psychology* (2016). https://doi.org/10.1177/1359105314536941

[42] Abraham H Maslow, Robert Frager, J Fadiman, C McReynolds, and R Cox. 1987. Motivation and personality (3rd). *New York* (1987).

[43] Mayoclinic. 2019. Mild cognitive impairment - Symptoms and causes - Mayo Clinic. (2019). https://www.mayoclinic.org/diseases-conditions/mild-cognitive-impairment/symptoms-causes/syc-20354578

[44] Rolf Molich and Jakob Nielsen. 1990. Improving a Human-computer Dialogue. *Commun. ACM* 33, 3 (mar 1990), 338–348. https://doi.org/10.1145/77481.77486

[45] Statistics Netherlands. 2019. Population Pyramid. (2019). https://www.cbs.nl/en-gb/visualisaties/population-pyramid

[46] Jakob Nielsen and Rolf Molich. 1990. Heuristic Evaluation of User Interfaces. In *Proceedings of the SIGCHI Conference on Human Factors in Computing Systems (CHI '90)*. ACM, New York, NY, USA, 249–256. https://doi.org/10.1145/97243.97281

[47] Maurice M Ohayon. 2004. Interactions between sleep normative data and sociocultural characteristics in the elderly. *Journal of Psychosomatic Research* 56, 5 (2004), 479–486. https://doi.org/10.1016/j.psychores.2004.04.365

[48] Carla M. Perissinotto, Irena Stijacic Cenzer, and Kenneth E. Covinsky. 2012. Loneliness in older persons: A predictor of functional decline and death. *Archives of Internal Medicine* 172, 14 (jul 2012), 1078–1083. https://doi.org/10.1001/archinternmed.2012.1993

[49] Andrea Poscia, Jovana Stojanovic, Daniele Ignazio La Milia, Mariusz Duplaga, Marcin Grysztar, Umberto Moscato, Graziano Onder, Agnese Collamati, Walter Ricciardi, and Nicola Magnavita. 2018. Interventions targeting loneliness and social isolation among the older people: An update systematic review. (feb 2018), 133–144 pages. https://doi.org/10.1016/j.exger.2017.11.017

[50] NitinB Raut, Sunitha Shanker, Shipra Singh, AlkaA Subramanyam, RavindraM Kamath, and Charles Pinto. 2014. Study of loneliness, depression and coping mechanisms in elderly. *Journal of Geriatric Mental Health* (2014). https://doi.org/10.4103/2348-9995.141920

[51] Jingshuang Shen, Chongyang Zhang, and Chuanwen Jiang. 2013. TV-Based Caring Videophone System for the Elderly in the Smart Home Environment. *Journal of Electrical and Computer Engineering* 2013, 2013 (2013). https://doi.org/10.1155/2013/651471

[52] Lais Soares Vello, Maria Alice Ornellas Pereira, and Regina Célia Popim. 2014. Mental health of the elderly: perceptions related to aging. *Investigación y Educación en Enfermería* 32, 1 (2014), 60–68. https://doi.org/10.1590/S0120-53072014000100007

[53] Statista. 2019. Niederlande - Durchschnittsalter der Bevölkerung bis 2050 | Statista. (2019). https://statista.extdb.e-fellows.net/statistik/daten/studie/214140/umfrage/durchschnittsalter-der-bevoelkerung-in-den-niederlanden/

[54] Andrew Steptoe, Natalie Owen, Sabine R Kunz-Ebrecht, and Lena Brydon. 2004. Loneliness and neuroendocrine, cardiovascular, and inflammatory stress responses in middle-aged men and women. *Psychoneuroendocrinology* 29, 5 (2004), 593–611. https://doi.org/10.1016/S0306-4530(03)00086-6

[55] Angelina R Sutin, Yannick Stephan, Martina Luchetti, and Antonio Terracciano. 2018. Loneliness and Risk of Dementia. *The Journals of Gerontology: Series B* (oct 2018). https://doi.org/10.1093/geronb/gby112

[56] Hatice Tel. 2013. Sleep quality and quality of life among the elderly people. *Neurology, Psychiatry and Brain Research* 19, 1 (feb 2013), 48–52. https://doi.org/10.1016/j.npbr.2012.10.002

[57] Robert Weiss. 1987. Reflections on the Present State of Loneliness Research. *Journal of Social Behavior and Personality* 2, 1 (1987), 1.

[58] WhatsApp. 2019. WhatsApp Features. (2019). https://www.whatsapp.com/features/

[59] Mi-Ra Won and Yun-Jung Choi. 2013. Are Koreans Prepared for the Rapid Increase of the Single-Household Elderly? Life Satisfaction and Depression of the Single-Household Elderly in Korea. *The Scientific World Journal* 2013 (2013). https://doi.org/10.1155/2013/972194

[60] Kathryn M Yorkston, Michelle S Bourgeois, and Carolyn R Baylor. 2010. Communication and aging. *Physical medicine and rehabilitation clinics of North America* 21, 2 (may 2010), 309–319. https://doi.org/10.1016/j.pmr.2009.12.011

YOUR KNOWLEDGE HAS VALUE

- We will publish your bachelor's and master's thesis, essays and papers

- Your own eBook and book - sold worldwide in all relevant shops

- Earn money with each sale

Upload your text at www.GRIN.com and publish for free